ISBN 978-0-578-29992-1

For information regarding permission, write Hood Heavenly, Permissions Team: 1660 S. University Drive #1047, Fort Worth, TX 76107

Published by Hood Heavenly

Printed in the U.S.A.

First Printing, 2022

VIRTUAL LEARNING

Virtual Learning

My Experience With Virtual Learning During A Pandemic

Nashiy Price

Hood Heavenly

The sky has never been the limit for an astronaut. It's just the beginning, and you're out of this world, kid.

~Love Dad

You were born to shine, Babygirl.
Never dim your light!

~Love Mom

VIRTUAL LEARNING
My Experience With Virtual Learning During A Pandemic
By Nashiy Price
COLORING BOOK
Designed by: Zoeyabara

My Village

Mommy: thank you for allowing me to be my creative self. To my da<
thank you for all of your encouragement. To Papa, Nana, Jaden,
Granny and Granddad, I love you all so much.

My Village

Mommy: thank you for allowing me to be my creative self. To my dad, thank you for all of your encouragement. To Papa, Nana, Jaden, Granny and Granddad, I love you all so much.

I miss my friends and can't wait to see them. Online school is the plac[e]
I'll meet and greet them.

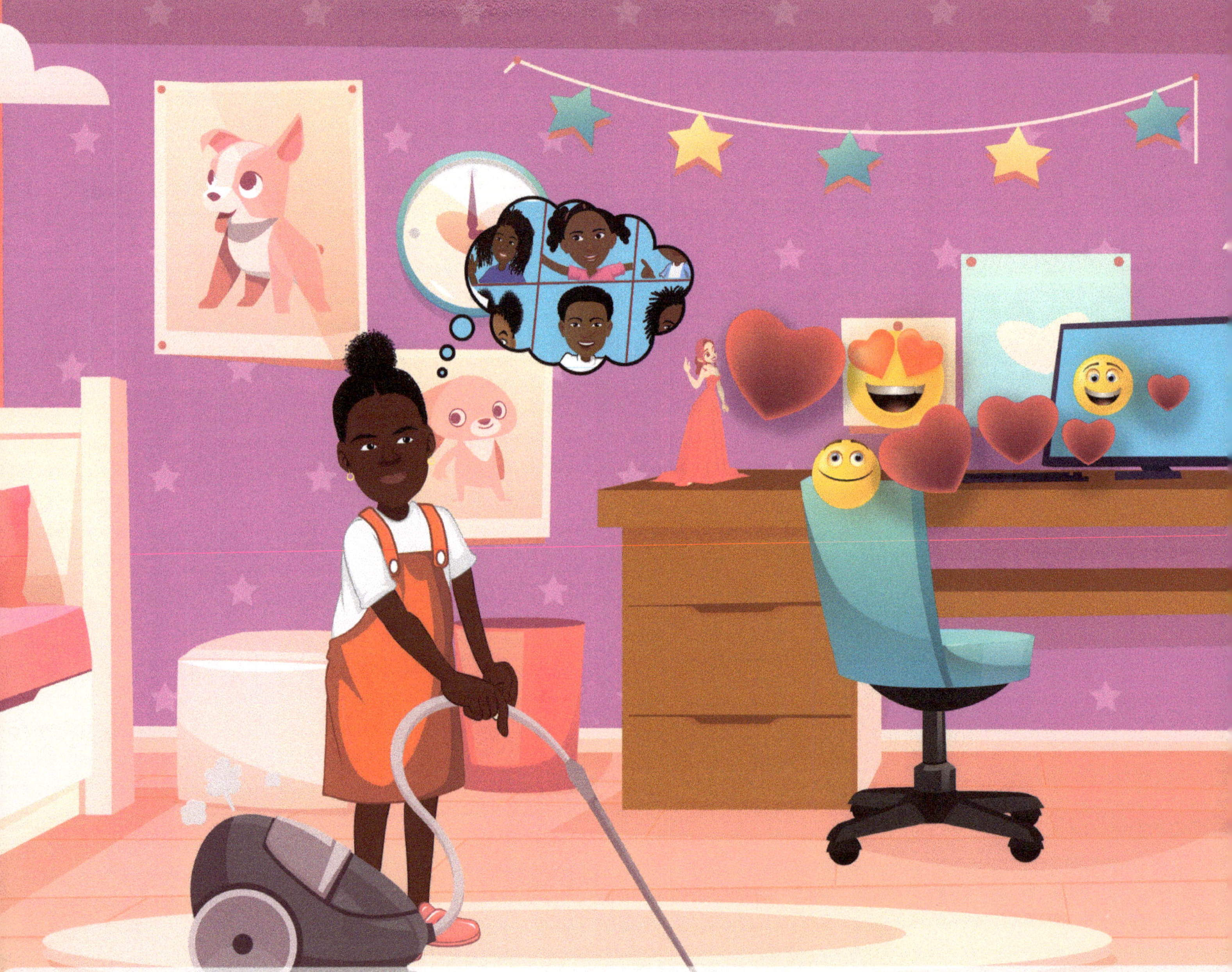

Lots of air hugs, smiley emojis, and happy faces. Virtual learning is fu[n]
and done at home, safe in our quiet spaces.

miss my friends and can't wait to see them. Online school is the place
I'll meet and greet them.

ots of air hugs, smiley emojis, and happy faces. Virtual learning is fun
and done at home, safe in our quiet spaces.

All the students and teachers must stay safe during this time. Social distancing and healthy choices are essential for us to shine.

Students can help their families stay safe, too. You can stay safe by washing your hands, wearing your face mask, and keeping your hand sanitizer close to you.

All the students and teachers must stay safe during this time. Social distancing and healthy choices are essential for us to shine.

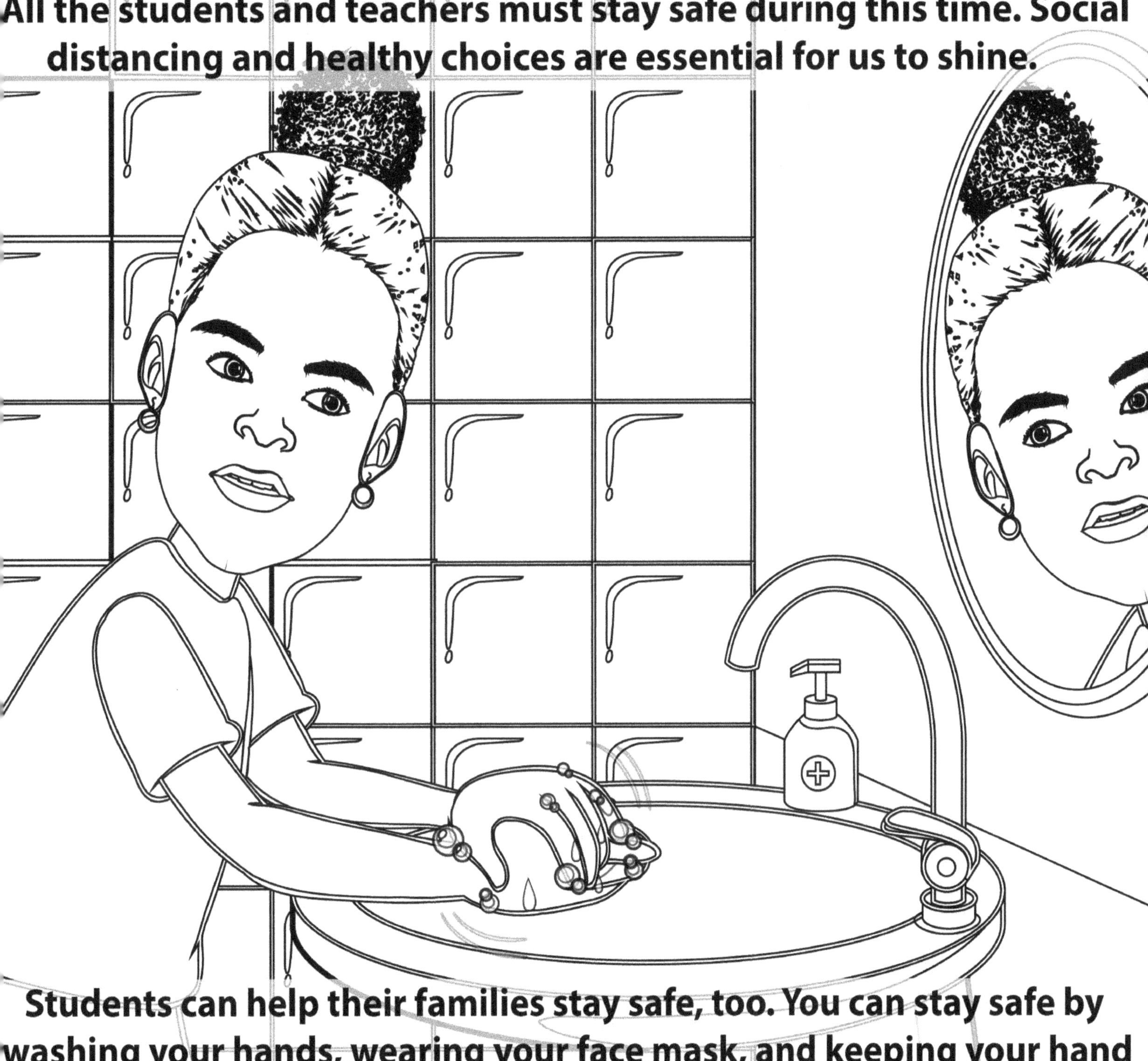

Students can help their families stay safe, too. You can stay safe by washing your hands, wearing your face mask, and keeping your hand sanitizer close to you.

I open my laptop to begin my day – zoom zoom. My teacher is ready and waiting for me virtually through Google Classroom.

My teacher teaches about reading, writing, social studies, and math.
Some of my classmates ask questions and pay attention,
and others, just laugh.

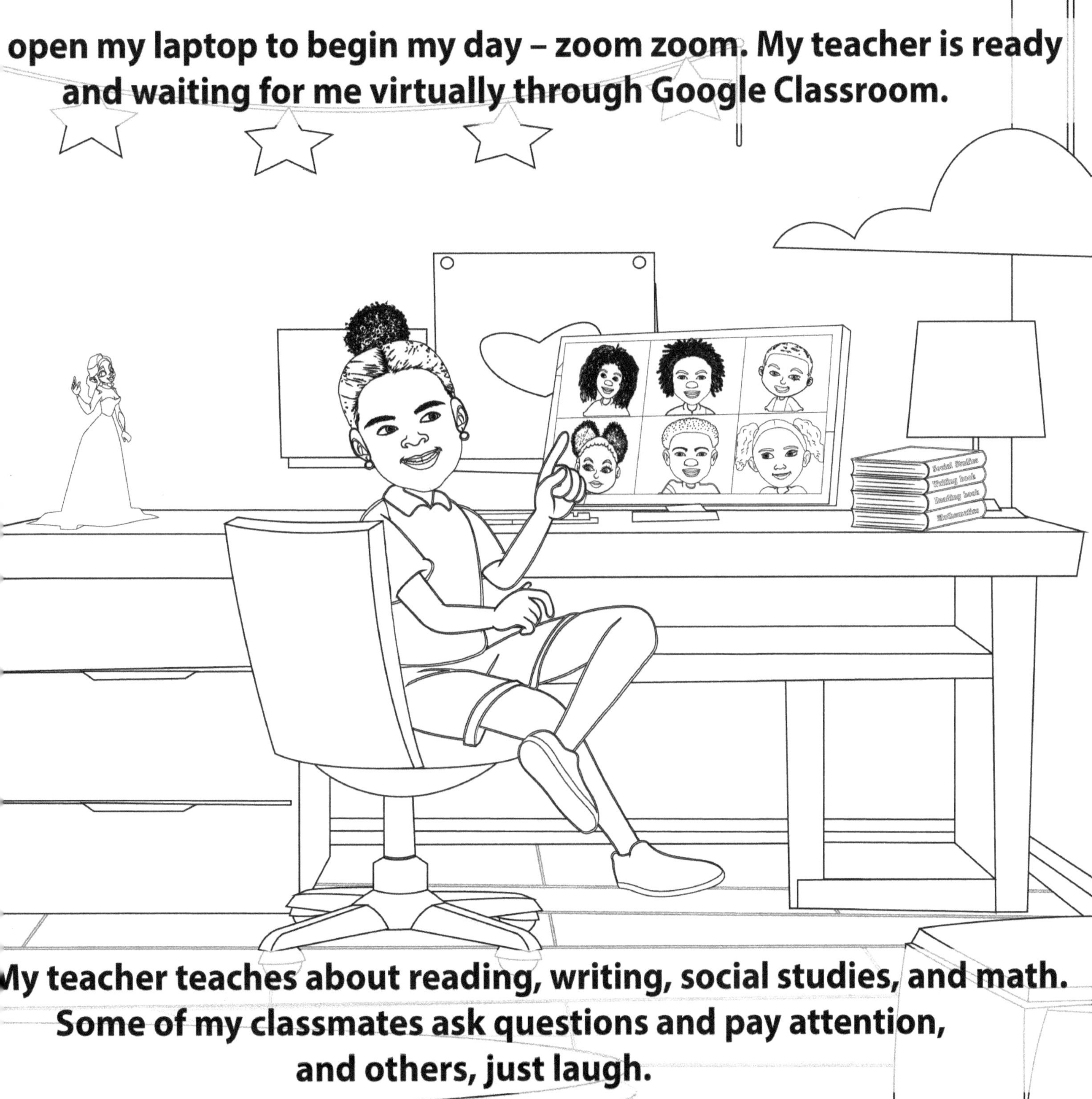

open my laptop to begin my day – zoom zoom. My teacher is ready and waiting for me virtually through Google Classroom.

My teacher teaches about reading, writing, social studies, and math. Some of my classmates ask questions and pay attention, and others, just laugh.

It is now time for lunch which is my favorite part of the day. Sandwich juice, and fruit all taste yummy from Mommy Kitchen Café.

is now time for lunch which is my favorite part of the day. Sandwich, juice, and fruit all taste yummy from Mommy Kitchen Café.

It's close to the end of the day, and time for me to turn in my assignments.
I double-check my classwork to make sure all is okay. Everything looks good, and I'm guaranteed a letter grade of A.

's close to the end of the day, and time for me to turn in my assignments.

I double-check my classwork to make sure all is okay. Everything looks good, and I'm guaranteed a letter grade of A.

I log in one more time to see my classmates and say goodbye. I sen
them many air hugs, smiley emojis, and happy faces.

Tomorrow morning, we will virtually learn again at home, in our quiet spac

I log in one more time to see my classmates and say goodbye. I send them many air hugs, smiley emojis, and happy faces.

Tomorrow morning, we will virtually learn again at home, in our quiet spaces.

Social Studies
Writing book
Reading book
Mathematics

The End